LUCKY MISFORTUNES

A Blueprint of a Personal Journey
Turning Pain Into Power

Alice Millen

Dedication

For my husband and children, who are the proof that the power of intention and visualization works. For my parents, who were the main reason why I felt the need to grow and move forward. And finally, to my deeply missed grandmother, who always believed in me, even when I didn't.

"Everytime I survive, only the weak part of me dies."

ALICE MILLEN

CONTENTS

INTRODUCTION

Overcoming a lifetime of adversities has helped me see that, with the right mindset, it is possible to transform pain into power. In Addition to many other "lucky misfortunes," for which I have now learned to be grateful, I have survived a nearly fatal accident, two heart attacks, bullying, and other setbacks. At one of life's crossroads, I decided to radically change my life and left my comfort zone, gave up a well-paid job, sold everything that didn't fit in my suitcase, and left for Australia on my own. With big dreams and a few belongings, I believed I had everything I needed within myself.

In this book, I am sharing a process for achieving goals and some coping strategies that helped me through the darkest days while starting over in life. I'm hoping that by reading this book, people who may be feeling trapped in limiting circumstances will be motivated to take steps towards a happier and more fulfilling life.

"Every time I survive, only the weak part of me dies." Alice Millen

1. RESILIENCE

Resilience is our ability to bounce back from adversities; it is also a powerful character builder.

Here is its Google definition: "The capacity to recover quickly from difficulties; toughness." I would remove the word quickly but keep the rest as it is.

However, if you search online for "resilient person," one of the definitions is: "Resilient people are aware of situations, their own emotional reactions, and the behaviour of those around them."

Another characteristic of resilience is the understanding that life is full of challenges. "While we cannot avoid many of these problems, we can remain open, flexible and willing to adapt to change."

From these definitions, we can understand how important it is to be resilient when trying to move forward after setbacks. Resilience is something that we can develop if we want to.

My upbringing in a dysfunctional family in Sao Paulo, Brazil, was very tough, and although it was hard to cope with living in fear from severe bullying by my father and feeling like an inconvenience for 16 years, I later came to understand that even that experience was a blessing in disguise.

Being bullied by a parent is something that can make or break a person. As a child, I didn't understand why he didn't like me. I would try to approach him, but he would get annoyed.

One day he told me I was like a little dog because whenever he would kick me in the butt, I would run back to him wagging my tail. I'm not sure how old I was, but after that, I never tried again.

I have no memory of ever receiving a compliment, a hug or any sign of affection from him. Instead, I have plenty of memories of him being horrible to me, beating me up, kicking me, shouting at me, and humiliating me for many years.

He always had keys in his pockets. I remember, when I was very young, being so scared that I would shiver and sometimes wet myself just from hearing the jingle of those keys as he walked.

My parents owned a fast food restaurant, and I used to work there; it was always very stressful when he was around, especially when he would push me or shout at me in front of the customers. It was particularly hard in my teenage years; I used to feel embarrassed. He really knew how to break me.

When I was 16, I had enough, so I asked my grandmother if I could live with her, and she kindly agreed; she actually saved me, as I don't know how long I would've been able to cope. I can't tell you how many times I wish I were never born.

He liked to remind me that I was stupid, and he often accused me of stealing money from them, which I swear on my children's lives I never did. He had a notebook where he wrote the serial number of some cash money and spread it around the house to see if I would steal it, so he could prove with his notes that it was his money.

When I got home from college one evening, he was waiting outside the gate; my heart sank when I saw him. He was furious, accusing me of stealing money from him.

Inside the house, he had made a huge mess, throwing and breaking things. He beat me up and shouted at me for a long time. He wouldn't believe me when I told him I didn't know about the money; he thought I was lying.

Later that night, my mum found the money underneath a plate in the cupboard, where he put it and forgot about it. He just took the money from my mum's hand and left. My father never apologised to me.

My mum has always been lovely and caring, but she wouldn't confront him. I am not sure if she was afraid of his violence or that he would leave her. None of them ever went to my grandmother's house to try to bring me back home. However, he said if one day I returned home drugged or pregnant, he would kick my butt away from there.

He thought so little of me; I never did anything to deserve such assumptions.

I think they were as relieved as I was when I moved out of that house. However, for many years after that, my father banned me from seeing my mother, and we had to arrange meetings in secret.

One day, during my lunch break from work, I went to their fast food place with three friends, as I knew he wouldn't be there at that time. My mum was really happy, and she made us some sandwiches and gave us some drinks.

We sat outside where they had some foldable tables and chairs, then my father came from nowhere and was furious to see me there.

He kicked the table so hard, everything fell on me and on my friends, then he went on to shout at me and push me away as if I were a stray dog. I was so embarrassed, but I had to take a bus and go back to work with my messy clothes and hair.

These are only a few examples of the bullying I suffered for all those years, and as you can imagine, I have too many of these horror stories to write them all down here.

The reason why I wanted to let you know about some of my experiences with my bully father is so that you understand how important my diaries and vision boards were at that time.

The vision of better days kept me going, and the pain fueled my determination to change my circumstances.

I don't want to sound sarcastic, but I am truly grateful for the sad years I lived with my parents, as I knew I never belonged there, and it taught me so much about the life I desired when I had my own family.

From 16 to 26 years old, I had my best years living with my grandmother. Her house was very small and humble, but it was perfect and peaceful; we were great company for each other, and I felt blessed to live ten happy years with her.

I will never forget my first night there. She treated me with so much love and respect that I finally felt welcome at home; it was a dream come true.

She was such a special person, extraordinarily kind, always funny and positive, hard-working until the last days of her life. She taught me so much, what a legend she was!

How can we build resilience?

If you research, you will find many ways, but I can only talk from my own experience.

This is what works for me:

1 - Take a step back and try to see the situation as if it were happening to someone else rather than yourself.

2 – Write down the advice you would give that person.

3 – Write everything that is hurting you on a piece of paper and

then burn it.

4 – Understand that whatever is making you suffer, is temporary.

5 – Say to yourself that you are already bouncing back.

6 - Ask what this situation is trying to teach you.

7 - Be grateful for being able to see the positive in darkness and for getting stronger.

8 – Switch your focus towards your goals.

9 – Practice mindfulness and be present in the present.

10 – Remember that emotions make things feel worse than they are; get practical.

11 – Make a plan to get out of that situation and follow it through.

12 – Look for inspiring stories about people who succeeded in what you are trying to achieve and follow their steps.

13 – Stick to your values and worth, do not accept less.

"Forgive those who didn't know how to love you. They were teaching you how to love yourself." Ryan Elliot

2. INTERESTING DISCOVERIES

I was amazed when I first heard about the power of intention, journaling and visualization because, without realising it, I have been more or less using these techniques since I was a child, but I had never thought about it as "a thing." Back then, my journals weren't very elaborate, but the concept was similar.

I used to write down many things that went through my mind, anything from silly thoughts to big ideas, and that would help me to get a better understanding of things that were important to me at times.

I am dyslexic, but I didn't know that until my adult life, so as you can imagine, my early years in school were challenging, and I had to find ways to make learning easier.

Text reading and comprehension have always been a struggle for me, but it is a different story when I write or when somebody else reads for me, as it gives me the chance to see a bigger picture outside my head.

It may not make much sense to a non-dyslexic person, and this isn't the subject of this book, but it does highlight the reason why I started journaling from a young age. My brain needs visual stimulation to understand things in the same way that other people would understand texts.

In the beginning, my journals and vision boards were about various things related to that moment in time, but now, so many years later, it is incredible to realize that many of those old dreams that sometimes seemed unreachable are part of my daily life, and for that I am forever grateful.

Vision boards and journaling really work; it is like having a recipe or a blueprint to follow, similar to a business plan or an architectural drawing, but customised to what you want to achieve in any area of your life, no matter how big or small.

Even if it sounds too good to be true, it actually works.

There are no mystical or magical tricks; it is purely and simply a well-designed step-by-step plan that you follow as you would follow a treasure map, and if you don't take any shortcuts, your treasure will be there waiting for you at the end.

What are your dreams?

Become rich, become healthier, win a competition, start a business, write books, or become president?

It really doesn't matter what it is, as long as it isn't something like winning the lottery, bringing people back from the dead, or having magical powers.

There is a process, and all you have to do is follow the steps that have been proved to work by all the successful people who you have ever heard about since the beginning of time.

When I talk about successful people, I don't mean only famous or very rich people.

I include everyone who has ever achieved something that they have prepared themselves for.

If you think about your current situation, can you honestly say that you are where you would like to be? If the answer is yes, then congratulations! You certainly worked really hard to get there, and you are probably still working hard to maintain yourself in that position, but to bring things back to reality, there is no surprise in achieving something that you prepared yourself for; it is more of a consequence than anything else.

Now, if the answer to this question is no, then you better make a decision.

Either accept things as they are, deal with the ups and downs, and STOP complaining.

Or do whatever it takes to achieve your goals.

There is no third option.

But hold on a minute!

Nobody said it would be easy or effortless, there are steps to follow, and here are some of them:

1 – Set an intention;

2 – Ask yourself why you want it;

3 – Hold a vision;

4 – Make a plan;

5 – Work on it one step at a time;

6 – Learn and enjoy the process;

7 – Reap the benefits.

Just as in a production line of a big factory, if you jump a step, the end product will be incomplete and faulty; it will fail the quality control and never reach the hands of a happy buyer.

If you work proactively towards a happier and more meaningful life, you will have to undertake and embrace change.

Humans are highly adaptable even in adverse circumstances; we become comfortable in the uncomfortable, which is why so many people go through their entire unfulfilled lives without even realising it.

A dream can be realised if you don't lose sight of your goal and persevere through the obstacles while moulding and shaping your being to accept and accommodate the changes and transformations that occur during the process.

Whether your motivation comes from pain or inspiration, the vision of change will empower you to use your energy and focus to achieve goals rather than avoid failure.

Take a step back to notice that you and your situation are two separate things, you are not defined by that; you are conditioned, and that is temporary until you take action.

"The best preparation for tomorrow is doing your best today" H. Jackson Brown Jr.

3. THOUGHT AWARENESS

When I was a child, I always had an "imaginary visual image" that was like a glass dome over me. Every time I was afraid of something, I'd imagine being protected by that dome.

Perhaps nowadays, children with that sort of imagination would think of something like a force field or a shield.

I felt safe in my dome; only good things could reach me, and all the bad things would stay out.

When I was breathing, I was breathing in courage and breathing out fear, so if there was any bad in me, it would leave and never come back.

I'm not sure how old I was when I created that dome, but I can honestly say that it still with me until this day, and I have attributed a few more powers to it as it can become stronger by absorbing great energy from others. I know it may sound a bit crazy, but the child with vivid imagination still lives in me, so whenever there is something scary, that's where I go, and I know it won't reach me; it is a place of calm.

Create your own imaginary shield all around you as if you had a force field, and feel confident that no harm from judgement or negativity will ever reach you.

Sometimes we can't avoid contact with some negative people, especially if they are family or a professional contact, but with the force field vision, you won't be affected by them.

Their problem is not with you; it is with them. They vibrate at a different frequency, so don't lower yours to receive theirs. They can only affect you if you allow them to, so be selective of the energy that you accept into your force field.

Another thing to be aware of is your choice of interests. Keep in mind that everything that you experience through any of your senses has an effect on your brain. It registers everything and translates it into chemicals that can either be helpful or harmful to your body and wellbeing.

Pay attention to your emotions. When you read some horrible news, watch a sad movie, or talk to someone who is in deep sorrow, although you may not have experienced the same sad event, through empathy you absorb that energy, and then your body chemicals change, making you feel stress and sadness in the same way.

I am not suggesting that you shouldn't have empathy, but I do want to highlight the importance of awareness. As long as you are protected by your "force field", it is OK to offer a shoulder to someone in need without allowing yourself to go down with them.

Be careful with what you choose to read, watch, and listen to, and try to stay away from problematic media content, gossip news, and other futile subjects.

There is plenty of good news in the world every day, but for some strange reason, great news is unlikely to attract the same amount of attention as all the bad news.

Seek out happy and enriching news, the kind that puts a smile on your face and instigates healthy curiosity, as it is a guaranteed source of feel-good hormones.

Make light, happy and interesting content choices to feed your thoughts, as they will affect your mood and how you feel about your day, and consequently your life.

The biggest transformations are the ones that come from within and once you go through that process, you will notice that many things that were part of your old self won't fit in with your new approach to life.

You need to protect your new position and perceptions, especially at the beginning when it is so easy to go back to your old ways.

Remember the dynamics of choice. You reason between alternatives, and let go of the ones that are no longer necessary or relevant.

It is advisable to reconsider what stays and what goes, and that includes relationships as well as old habits.

Now that you know the importance of thought awareness and how costly or profitable it can be, learn to filter what type of energy you allow into your life.

Do whatever you can to reduce stress, cut off toxic interactions, negative energy, and bad environments.

By now, I hope you feel confident enough to start a revolution in your life, and I purposely used the word "revolution" because that's exactly what it is.

It all starts with a decision, which must be followed by action. If you do so, you will take charge of your life and make time for working on your goals by reorganising your priorities within and around you.

You are entitled to your own life management; nobody will come to save you from your aspirations. You either act on pursuing your dreams and goals or they will keep on haunting you wherever you go, as you will always be reminded of your desires whether you work to achieve them or not.

Perhaps that's why some refer to it as "your calling in life" or "purpose in life."

Here, in this book, you have all the necessary tools to guide you through the steps, but for this process to work, the most important part is you and your commitment to follow them through.

Equally important is your commitment to open your mind to new concepts and positively embrace all challenges and changes, regardless of how hard it may be.

You don't need to believe me, as none of the principles and techniques in this book are new. They have been around for a long time, some longer than others, as you can see from the works of Socrates and Aristotle to those of Napoleon Hill and other philosophers from more recent times.

They all seemed to agree that our greatest power and weakness are in our minds.

Believe that you can succeed; set goals; make plans;work hard; and give your best at all times. Maintain your focus and continue to lear and improve. Stay strong when things go wrong; resist defeat, be patient, persist, and carry on only to rest when you get where you aim to be.

When you reach your goal, you will be on top of the world, with all the qualities of a great warrior. No matter what it is that you have achieved, the satisfaction is on you.

The skills that you acquire in the journey of pursuing your goals will elevate your being, and once you have that in you, the process is the same for any other goal that you decide to achieve.

Many will realize that in the end, the journey was just as amazing as the achievement of the goal itself, if not more so, because of what who became in the process.

"The secret of change is to focus all of your energy, not on fighting the old but on building the new" Socrates

4. CONSCIOUS TRANSFORMATION

N ow that we covered the principles of thought awareness, it is opportune to talk about conscious transformation.

To illustrate the point, I first need to give you a bit of background:

At the beginning of 2016, I had a serious health issue that nearly killed me. I survived two heart attacks at the age of 43 due to SCAD (Spontaneous Coronary Artery Dissection), a relatively rare heart condition that I didn't know I had and knew nothing about until that day.

It didn't happen because of plaque build-up or any of the traditional risk factors for cardiac disease. For some strange reason, one of the arteries in my heart decided to tear apart and cause all the trouble.

To say the least, it was a life-changing experience from which I am still recovering, and I'd like to highlight that the body heals way faster than the mind.

After a heart attack, we hear a lot about getting used to "a new normal," and for a long time, I felt sorry for myself and sometimes angry and frustrated for not having much energy and for being too scared to even step out of bed. Every day was a struggle; I was missing out on enjoying my life and, even worse, I was missing out on enjoying my family as I just couldn't keep up.

Before the heart attacks, I had always been active, healthy and reasonably fit, so it was my first time experiencing an inconsistency between my mind and body. I was feeling as if I had an empty battery.

Nobody knows why SCAD happens, and for that reason, there isn't a cure or preventive treatment.

I was terrified that it could happen again, so for two years, I developed new habits to fit with my new normal, spending more time sleeping than being awake, and I avoided anything that, in my opinion, could cause more harm to my heart. I started to feel depressed and "protected" myself from too much excitement.

Meanwhile, I was always trying to get better, as I am naturally a positive person, and this "new normal" didn't feel right to me.

I started to think, and while reasoning with myself, I acknowledged that this wasn't the first time I had escaped death, and it wasn't the worst experience I had ever had in life either.

Therefore, I refused to be defined by that, so I started fighting back, and from then on, things started to change.

At any given opportunity, I was always researching and learning about people who overcame limitations and went on to live a better life than before their "event," as they refer to a heart attack.

It didn't take much for me to get inspired, and I set up a goal to transform my new normal into a better normal, although I still didn't have the energy I had had in the past.

"Just when the caterpillar thought her life was over, she became a butterfly." Barbara Haines Howett

I had been practising most of the ideas from this book long before the heart problems, so I reckon that my recovery had a strong starting point. However, I truly believe that it can help anyone who is willing to put in the effort towards self-improvement in any area of their lives, regardless of how far along they are in their journey.

In my case, for my own recovery, I just followed the advice in this book by setting-up some goals, working on acquiring new habits, and learning from admirable people who managed to succeed after going through similar experiences, and then continuing to work every day on thought awareness, gratitude, and affirmations.

I had to work very hard on my mental strength before I could feel the strength building up in my body, and then I learned about the concept of 'affirmations' and how powerful they can be.

I had heard about it before but had never practised it as I am a sceptical person who needs to understand the logic behind things, especially if they sound a bit "magical."

At first I was suspicious, but then I noticed that so many intelligent and respectful people were endorsing it, and since I had nothing to lose, I decided to give it a try just to see if all that noise was valid.

It felt hypocritical to start with; there I was saying to myself in the mirror that I was feeling great while my inner voice, which isn't very polite or subtle, was telling me, "No, you're not; stop being ridiculous."

The principles underlying affirmations are similar to those for visualisation, with which I was already familiar, but instead of picturing what you want to achieve in the future, you express acknowledgement and gratitude for feelings that you want to experience in the present as if you already have them.

I had to fight to ignore my negativity, as it was hard to convince myself that I was feeling great when my body was failing to store energy.

Then I learned that the secret was to focus on the positive, even if it was hard to find, and also to reinforce my gratitude.

Here is an example to illustrate how I did it:

Instead of focusing on how tired and dizzy I was or dwelling on feeling guilty for not interacting much with my family and friends, I would intentionally take my resting moments to practise mindfulness, thought awareness, affirmations, and gratitude.

Mindfulness encourages you to be 'present in the present', with no judgements. You just pay attention to your feelings and thoughts while deliberately breathing in and out.

In thought awareness I would debate with my negative thoughts and substitute them with positive and encouraging thoughts.

When I was resting on my bed midweek in the afternoon, instead of listening to my nasty inner voice saying that I was being lazy while my husband was working so hard to bring money home, or that I would die and miss out on seeing my children grow up, I decided to listen to my kind inner voice saying that I should give my body the rest it needed to be able to recover and rebuild its strength.

For affirmation, I would say things like:

"My body is strong and healthy, my heart is healed;

I feel great and energized, I choose to only think positively."

For gratitude I would say that I was thankful for another chance at life and for the privilege of re-evaluating my priorities.

Some opportunities come disguised as misfortunes. Many times in life I have been battered so badly by circumstances that I could literally feel soul-crushing pain, but apart from losing my grandmother without having the chance to say goodbye, I must say that I am grateful for all the times I have been knocked off my feet, as all these experiences made me who I am today.

By making a conscious decision, I bounced back once again and now I see everything as a blessing for the eye-opening opportunities that always come with my setbacks.

I regained confidence in my body to keep on pushing it to achieve more, although it is still a work in progress. I can honestly say that my life is better now than it has ever been, and the main reason for that is my shift in perception as a result of my efforts and input.

I decided that every time I survive, only the weak part of me dies.

You can't change what happened to you, but you can always choose how you allow it to affect you. The sooner you break the chains of victim mentality, the sooner you start to reclaim your strengths and get back to the game with more determination to win.

Be grateful for hardships, as they are helpful in instigating growth, redirection, focus, and re-evaluation of priorities.

Be grateful for your growing pains; they will leave scars, some deeper than others, but wear them proudly as a reminder of a battle that didn't defeat you.

This practice still helps me today.

Not having to deal with feeling guilty for resting when my body needs it has been liberating, as it has become a precious time when I recharge my batteries.

This practise has become a habit, and I no longer need to make an effort to focus on the positive side of things. Of course, some days are harder than others, but in general, they are all great, as I recognise how lucky I am to be alive.

Now I experience feelings with much more intensity just because I am present in the present and aware of my thoughts, and I am again grateful for every day that comes as I know how close I was to not having them anymore.

Shifting your perception is a key factor in recovering from all sorts of problems, as if you are in good mental health, it will be reflected in your physical health.

The affirmations can be spoken, written, thought, sung, or presented in any other way that you feel comfortable with.

Since my mindset shift, I have been consciously practising these techniques every night before bed, together with a little prayer, and then again in the morning before stepping out of bed. I remind myself of my vision and break it down into daily actions towards my goals. This is my own little ritual, which I have learned to enjoy.

If you are sceptical, as I am, there are numerous scientific studies in this field, and for self-affirmation references, you may want to search for: Claude Steele, Sander L. Koole, Batia M. Wiesenfeld, and many others.

By repeating positive phrases to yourself, they will start manifesting in the subconscious mind as easily and frequently as the negative thoughts do.

It is fascinating that the mind can be trained as much as the body to perform tasks and behaviours.

Emotional intelligence is an overlooked subject that, in my opinion, is so important that it should be taught in schools from the very early years.

It is related to awareness of personal and social emotions and their effects in thoughts and actions.

Wouldn't it be great to learn how to act upon emotions and how to benefit from understanding them?

The transition from childhood to adulthood is very well supported in the areas of intellectual development, while little attention is spent on the emotional side.

The cumulative effect of not knowing how to recognise and manage emotions may cost you dearly later in life when some people make poor decisions based on their overwhelming frustrations.

I believe the world would be a better place if people had a more conscious and intelligent use of their emotions.

"We become what we think about." Earl Nightingale

5. START JOURNALING

A journal is a place for you to register and keep track of your thoughts, ideas, plans and experiences; it is a way to externalize what goes inside the mind. Find a notebook or something similar to be used as a journal.

For the purpose of demonstration, let's create a journal for a couple of simple and reasonably short-term examples:

Suppose that your dream is to have a better position at work or lose weight or even both things.

Well, I must say that for each dream you will need a separate plan; remember, there are no shortcuts!

The first step for each and every dream is to **have an intention**, which means that you hold that idea in your head, and it feels good to imagine yourself in that position.

You probably already know what it should look like, but before you start thinking about the many reasons why it would be too difficult or even impossible, you will need to ask yourself some important questions:

What is my main dream?

Why do I want it?

Your answers should reflect what you want for yourself and not what others want or expect from you.

In this sense, this is a lonely journey of self-improvement and growth, you can't do this for others, and nobody can do it for you.

If your answers to the above questions don't reflect what you want for yourself, then you need to stop right there and **choose your own dream.**

TASK 1:

If this is your own dream, then please write down what it is:

Now it is time to transform your dream into a goal.

For illustration, here are our examples again:

Dream: Have a better position at work.

This is too vague; you need to be very specific and change it to the actual position that you want to have and give it a time frame.

Goal: Become a Marketing Director at (company's name) by __/ __/__.

Reasons why:

- Earn more money
- Work fewer hours
- Get involved in creative processes
- Be in charge
- Have status
- Wear smart clothes
- Learn new skills
- Kiss my boss goodbye
- Travel for business
- Meet important people

At this stage, don't worry if that time frame seems too soon or too far, as you work on the next steps and get a better understanding of what you need to do, you will be able to adjust it accordingly.

Onto our next example:

Dream: Lose weight

Again, be very specific about what you really want to achieve.

This is better:

Goal: Lose 20 Kg in 3 months, from __/__/__ to __/__/__.

Reasons why:

- Be healthier
- Wear sexy clothes
- Eat better food
- Wear size 10
- Don't feel embarrassed about my body
- Feel beautiful
- Enjoy exercising
- Be more confident

The list of reasons for each goal can be as long or short as you wish.

Use bullet points to each one, it will help you later when you need to go back to them.

Continue to ignore the negative thoughts that may appear and carry on writing even if some ideas seem absurd or foolish. This is a brainstorm and when you are in that "zone", all ideas are welcome.

What you **can't** do is sabotage the list and choose which ideas to include.

Remember, now isn't the time to judge.

Another thing that I would like to mention is that your dreams and goals don't need to be very fancy; they could be something like, run a marathon, become a better friend or learn to swim.

This is a process that can be applied to just about anything.

TASK 2:

I would like to suggest that you use the blank spaces provided to transform your dream into a specific goal, followed by the reasons why you want it.

Until you get used to this process, it is better to have only one goal.

Later, you will agree with me that it is better to dedicate your full attention and focus on one thing at a time, or it will get too hard to keep track of so many things all at once.

So, back to your list.

Again, this is brainstorming; all ideas are welcome, you will have a chance to choose and trim them later.

Let your inner voice speak to you, do not judge or censure it.

Just remember to be specific!

Dream:

Goal:

Reasons why:

"If you want to live a happy life, tie it to a goal, not to people or objects." Albert Einstein

6. HOLD A VISION

Now that you've completed your list, proceed without hesitation to create a vision board for the one specific goal you chose for this task.

Holding a vision of what you want to achieve gives you the possibility to materialise your ideas and to get used to that reality before it happens.

What is a vision board?

It is a simple picture collage that holds images related to your goal.

There isn't a right or wrong way to do this, you can create it by cutting pictures from magazines, using photos from the internet, drawing it yourself, adding quotations, and literally anything you want in any shape or size.

To choose your images, pick some that illustrate the looks, feelings and experiences as if you had already achieved the goal.

This step may seem unnecessary or childish, but when you think about someone building a house without drawings, you will have a better understanding of its importance.

Consider that all man-made things you see in around you were once inside someone's head. From the tallest buildings to the buttons on your shirt, everything started with an idea, then became an intention, which grew into an image, and then kept on following the process until it took its physical form.

What is the importance of a vision board?

It is a powerful form of motivation with visual impact that helps you to keep focused, reminding you of where you want to be. It shows you how it is going to look and feel, so you can get used to that reality when you get there.

What do you do before you go on holiday?

You search for a place, you look at pictures, you read reviews, and look at where it is. When the time comes, if you did your research properly, you won't end up in a different place, but if you do, you will still know which direction to take to get to the right place.

Vision boards have the same purpose. They are like maps of where you are going, and you will recognise when you get there because you know what it should be like.

If you don't know where you are going, how do you know when you get there? (inspired by Lewis Carroll's quote)

Where should I keep my vision board?

Place it where you can see it every day for as long and as often as possible.

If your goal is related to work, it could be on the wall at your workplace or used as a screen saver for your computer.

If it is related to personal development, it could be on your bedroom ceiling or any other place that won't be hidden from your sight for too long.

Visual stimulus is very impactful, and every time you look at the board, you will feel inspired and more commited to your goal.

The science indicates that visuals cause involuntary reactions as your body produces feel-good hormones and endorphins every time you look at things that make you happy.

Now that you understand the importance of a vision board and realise that you can't escape this step, you better get prepared to start with yours.

Here are two vision boards to illustrate the examples of goals mentioned earlier. Remember, this is just a suggestion, **you may like to do yours in a different way, and that is totally fine.**

There are, however, a few observations about the choice of words and colours that you want to display on your vision board.

Try not to use negative words, even if they are part of a positive context.

On the examples below, we have some wonderful motivational quotes, but they contain negative words.

As the vision board will also communicate with your subconscious mind, you need to take into consideration the energy of each word individually.

On our examples, I used some of my favourite motivational quotes, but notice that they contain the words NOT, RISK, DON'T, CAN'T, LOST and there are also some words in red that our brain may unconsciously associate with a "STAY AWAY" signal.

You can still use any quotation that you choose, but you may like to substitute the negative words with positive synonyms and rearrange or rewrite the sentences in a way that maintains the essence of the initial message.

Compare the vision boards below and notice how slight changes make a big difference.

Did you notice the difference?

There are so many ways to say the same thing, but please let's make it clear that there is nothing wrong with the original quotations; in fact, they are fantastic. However, for the purpose of our vision board, negative words would be better left out.

TASK 3:

Since you have transformed your dream into a goal and learned the principles for an effective vision board, use this opportunity to practice creating the vision board for **your main goal**.

Remember, only one at a time.

Ideally, it is better to use a loose sheet of paper so you can place it where you can see it as often as possible.

"Hold the vision, trust the process" Unknown Author

7. BE SPECIFIC

It is time to go back to your bullet-point list of reasons for wanting your goal. Please read each line out loud.

In doing so, you will feel the energy of your reasons. It may give you goosebumps, but don't worry if it doesn't, you will have plenty of opportunities to feel the energy later.

For illustration, I'll copy and paste our examples here so I can explain the next steps, but you don't need to copy yours, you can simply return to that page and work on it from there.

You will revise and trim your ideas, make sure they are very specific and straight to the point, and leave no room for misinterpretation.

It will be clearer with the examples, so here we go:

First example

Goal: Become a Marketing Director at (company's name) by __/__/__.

Reasons why:

- Earn more money

How much is the salary for that position in your company and at their competitors?

If you know, you will need to change the line "EARN MORE

MONEY" and put down the actual amount that you want to earn together with a time frame.

Like this:

"EARN (x amount) PER YEAR"

If you don't know how much that is, you will need to find out by researching the market for that position in your area.

You can't expect to achieve something without knowing what that something is.

- Work fewer hours

How many hours would you like to work?

Change that line to "WORK (x number) HOURS PER WEEK.

- Get involved in creative processes

This one is good as it is

- Be in charge

In charge of what or whom?

A specific project, a team, a department, an area?

- Have status

You may like to be more specific and change this line to something like "GAIN & MAINTAIN SOCIAL STATUS"

- Wear smart clothes

For work, all the time or special occasions?

- Learn new skills

This one is good as it is, but you may like to narrow it a bit more in case you know which skills you would like to learn.

- Kiss my boss goodbye

I guess you don't want to literally kiss your boss goodbye, so you could change this line for something like "Respond to x boss", "Be transferred to x department" or "Become the boss of my boss".

- Travel for business

Occasionally or regularly?

Locally or internationally?

- Meet important people

Who? A specific person or a group of people?

The revised list of reasons for our first example looks like this:

- Earn (x amount) per year
- Work (x number) hours per week
- Get involved in creative processes
- Be in charge of (x department)
- Gain & maintain social status
- Wear smart clothes for work and upgrade my personal wardrobe
- Learn new marketing skills
- Become part of the executive management team for (area x)
- Travel for work occasionally both locally and internationally
- Meet influential and like-minded people from senior management

Onto our second example:

Goal: Lose weight

Again, be very specific about what you really want to achieve.

Go direct to the point:

Goal: Lose 20 Kg in 3 months, from __/__/__ to __/__/__.

Reasons why:

- Be healthier

This is a great reason; however, you could give it a deeper and more embracing meaning.

- Wear sexy clothes

There is nothing wrong with this one, so we will leave it as it is.

- Eat better food

What do you consider better food?

Tastier?

Healthier?

Organic?

Gluten-free?

Something else?

- Wear size 10

Another one that we can leave as it is because it is a clear and direct reason.

- Don't feel embarrassed about my body

I would combine this one with "Feel beautiful" and "Be more confident" because they are very similar, and if you became more confident, you will solve all three with one shot.

- Feel beautiful

This will come as a consequence.

- Enjoy exercising

For you to enjoy doing something you don't really like, you will have to work on your mental strength to develop new habits.

We will talk about it later in this book, but for now, it would be more appropriate to narrow it down a bit more.

- Be more confident

About what?

Your body?

Your personality?

Both?

Something else?

Expand and analyse each reason.

The revised list for our second example looks like this:

Goal: Lose 20 Kg in 3 months, from __/__/__ to __/__/__.

Reasons why:

- Have a healthier lifestyle
- Wear sexy clothes
- Eat healthier and wholesome food
- Wear size 10
- Become self-confident
- Develop the habit of enjoying exercising

TASK 4:

Revise your bullet point list for wanting your goal and change the reasons that aren't specific.

Make them undoubtedly clear and direct.

You may be asking if you should leave out the ones that seem impossible, and the answer to that is a big, fat NO!

Specific list of reasons for wanting my goal:

"You miss 100% of the shots you don't take." Wayne Gretzky

8. GET TO THE CORE

Now that your list of reasons for wanting your goal is straight to the point, you will ask yourself what is needed for each idea to become reality.

You will keep on asking and answering until every single one has been narrowed down to its core.

This process can be lengthy, laborious and involves a lot of research.

Negative and contrary thoughts may arise, and if they do, you will need to find solutions for them too, but don't panic; **you can do it!**

Write the answers as they are and not how you would like them to be, keeping in mind that this is between you and yourself.

Nobody is judging, and cheating would be a waste of your own time.

At the end of this step, you will have a plan of action for you to follow, and that is going to be your treasure map.

There is a reason why so many people never achieve their goals, it takes a lot of hard work.

Graphics always work wonders for my dyslexic brain, but you don't need to use them if you prefer a different way. As long as you are able to dissect your reasons to their core, any way is fine.

Let's start analysing our examples in more depth.

To make it easier to understand, the required skills from our example were separated into three categories, "Personal", "Academic" and "Professional".

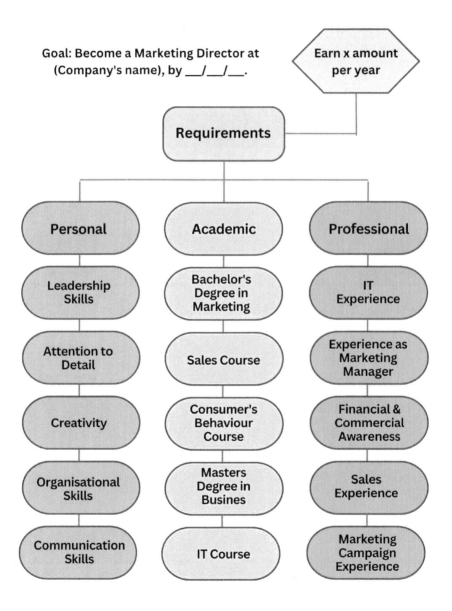

After categorising the requirements, you can put each one through the process chart, which will leave you with another three groups:

"Acquire", "Improve" or "You got it".

You will repeat this process to all requirements for the goal you are aiming to achieve.

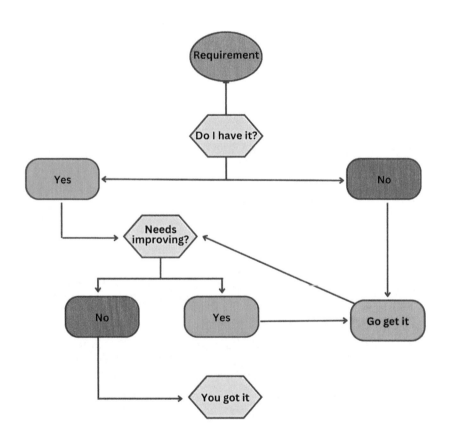

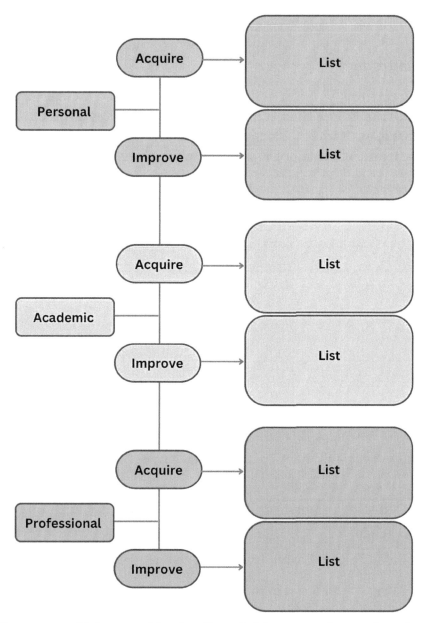

Now you will leave aside the list of things you have already put together and get busy working on your two other lists: the list of the things you already have but need to improve and the list of things you need to acquire.

Again, we will need to narrow them down in order to have absolute certainty of which direction to take to avoid wasting time and money.

Take your time; you can always come back to it if you think you have exhausted the theme. **There is no deadline; you can choose your pace, but remember that the time will pass whether you do it or not, and at some point you will wish you had started now.**

This book is not about teaching people to become marketing directors or to lose weight. It is about the process of achieving goals, and for that reason, I won't go into any more details of the topics left in the "Acquire" and "Improve" lists. However, I will still explain them and the further steps that must be taken in more general terms.

The personal skills that you need to improve or acquire will be better explained later when you pick and choose the character traits that you want to have and work on them from all aspects.

The academic and professional skills will need to be put through the process again, until you can pinpoint what you have to work with.

Once again you will need to do one at a time.

Let's say that, from the academic list, you need to acquire a master's degree in business, but there are three reasons stopping you:

"You can't afford it, haven't got the time and can't travel".

Now we must find ways to make it possible.

"The man on top of the mountain didn't fall there." Vince Lombardi

TASK 5:

Take your list of things to acquire and improve and use the space below to make a list with as many possibilities as you can think of, the more the merrier.

Here is another process chart that you may like to use:

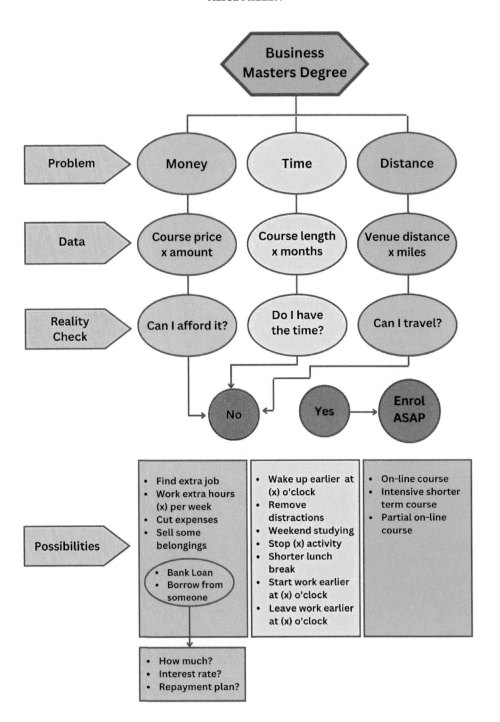

Now that you know what you have to do to acquire or improve the missing skills, just repeat this process whenever necessary.

What if I don't believe the goal-achieving process described in this book?

Then it won't work for you, as it only works for those who are open and willing to embrace the challenge and committed to follow the steps.

All successful people that you can think about have taken their own steps to get where they are and have prepared themselves to keep their position.

If success was a currency, preparation would be its value.

What if I think it will be too difficult or take too long?

Then you probably don't want it that much; these are excuses for not taking action.

Just don't wait too long, as your life is happening now, and the time will pass even if you don't take action.

Unless you have a plan to do things differently, your future will look just like your past, as you can't continue to do things the same way and expect different results.

"The definition of insanity is doing the same thing over and over again and expecting a different result." Albert Einstein

9. REALITY CHECK

Now you have a well-defined goal that you want to achieve and a list of steps to work with – Consider this your plan of action.

While some people will be excited to proceed with the steps straight away, others will freeze right there, thinking that although it all sounds great, they still can't do it.

If you belong to the second group, the good news is that, **yes, you can do it too**, but first you need to work on your limiting beliefs that are holding you back and differentiating you from the "go get" group.

In your understanding, what is keeping you in that position?

Let's get personal and write a list of reasons why you don't think you are able to proceed.

For illustration, let's pick a few made-up reasons:

Fear of failure
Fear of judgment
Lack of self-confidence
Lack of confidence in this process
It will take too long time
Too much effort

It is a natural thing to fear failure, and for most of the reasons above, that is ok. In fact, it would be very strange if we were fearless at all times, as fear is part of human nature.

A degree of fear is healthy and helps us to be cautious with our choices; we fear because we don't want to get hurt, lose money, waste time, disappoint others and so on.

What is not ok is for you to be paralyzed by these fears.

It is important to analyse and separate real fear from lack of willingness to change habits, behaviours and convenient excuses.

It is much easier to claim that the lack of progress is due to fear, than acknowledging that you are just making excuses, since there is far less guilt and responsibility involved.

What is fear?

If you Google it, here is one of the definitions that comes up at the top of the page:

"An unpleasant emotion caused by the threat of danger, pain, or harm."

If you are trying to protect yourself from getting hurt, how can the reality of never fulfilling your dream be less painful?

When we confront our fears, it is important to accept that they only exist in our imagination. They are the result of the brain imagining the worst-case scenarios, the annoying "what ifs".

Why is that we always think the worst?

Because it gives us comfort to have reasons for justifying our decision to stay where we are, as it is safe and reasonably comfortable.

But is it really comfortable or even safe, or is it just familiar and manageable?

If you feel frustrated about your position in relation to your dream, it is definitely not comfortable.

Is it safe then?

Well, it depends on your perception of safety. If the frustration of not having what you want makes you depressed, sad, or even uneasy, the answer is that you are not safe as these unwanted feelings can make you ill and resentful in the long run.

Later in life, you don't want to look back and realise how much being too cautious has cost you.

Don't put yourself in the position of regretting things you haven't done.

What if you go ahead and succeed instead?

Remember, "what if" never happened; it only exists in your head, so why not reverse it into a positive scenario instead?

If everything goes wrong, you can always go back to where you are, or you can take the lesson and try again in a different way, and eventually you will succeed as your chances get higher the more you try.

Can I still fail?

Yes, but if you think that no failure comes without a lesson, this fail was already better than the failure of not trying.

Fear of failure is already a failure if it stops you.

"The only thing we have to fear is fear itself." Franklin D. Roosevelt

If you think your goal is too difficult and for that reason you wouldn't try, then your problem is not ; it is lack of willingness and commitment.

For reference, there are so many great stories that we can learn from. Just to mention a few, search for the biography of Walt Disney, Einstein, or Henry Ford.

You are likely to change your mind when you learn about their journey and stop thinking that your goal is too difficult to achieve.

Yes, it's difficult, but it's also as doable as you make it.

People and ideas are like little seeds; we start small and fragile but so did the mighty oak trees; in the right environment and conditions, every seed has the potential to become more, and that applies to all beings and their endeavours.

We are in this world for a limited amount of time, and we were made for achieving great things or we wouldn't be blessed with creativity and intelligence, so let's get busy doing what we can to unlock our full potential.

Do your best at any task that you agree to take on, however big or small. Always offer more than is expected from you, and do it with pride and commitment. Make a reputation for yourself that, whatever you do, it is done to the best of your ability; you can't do more than your best, and that should be enough.

What if I give my best but it still isn't enough?

Who is judging?

Yourself, or others?

If you are self-judging and you are sure you have given your best, you will know that even if you didn't reach the expected outcome, it wasn't due to lack of effort and commitment on your part, and yes, it was enough.

Self-judgment is an expression of the mind, a little voice that most often speaks to us uninvitedly and has two sides: the positive and the negative.

On the one hand, it can be a wonderful tool for self-improvement, or it can be a dangerous suppressive shadow sitting on our shoulders preventing us from shining.

However, our brain is like a garden, the thoughts you feed and look after will thrive, so practise focusing on the positive thoughts more than the negative ones.

It is usually easier to listen to negative thoughts as they have the excuse of protecting us; they want to prevent us from trying new things, while they actually steal opportunities and experiences from us.

Remember that you are the boss of your mind, and whatever you decide goes. Beware of your thoughts, and create the habit of finding a positive thought for every negative that comes in. Take control by confronting and questioning.

Back to our example, let's say that you have acquired everything you need to apply for the job you want, but your mind keeps putting you down by saying that you aren't good enough, that you will make a fool of yourself, or that such a high-calibre position is not for you.

The best way to get over these negative thoughts that seem so real and terrifying is to debate them.

You may like to do it mentally or verbally, but I'll show you how to do it visually, and you can decide which way works better for you.

I'd make a list of the negative thoughts as they come, and then write positive thoughts to confront them as if in a dialogue between myself and my mind.

We are used to thinking in a certain way. The negative thoughts can be very nasty, but we don't dare to confront them because we don't think of them as being separate from ourselves.

This exercise will help you to be aware of your thoughts, face your fears, and remind you that the scenario is unreal; it never happened outside of your mind.

For example:

Self: Now that I have all that is necessary to apply for the job, why don't I just do that?

Mind: Don't be ridiculous; you won't be chosen.

Self: Why ridiculous and why not?

Mind: Who do you think you are, there are lots of people applying who may be better than you.

Self: I am not ridiculous; in fact, I am brilliant because I worked really hard to acquire the skills for this position and I am prepared for it.

Mind: Don't bother trying, you won't get the job.

Self: I'll try, and if I don't get it, I'll keep on trying until I do.

By confronting these thoughts and practising opposite affirmations, they will eventually lose their strength while you decide how much power you want to give to them.

This practice will shift your energy into a lighter and more confident position, which is helpful while you work on developing the habit of taking control of your thoughts.

What if I fear being judged by others?

Then here is a list of questions for you to ask yourself:

1 - Who are these people?

( ) Family,
( ) Friends,

( ) Romantic Partner,
( ) Professional Contact,
( ) Neighbours, Community
( ) People on Social Media,
( ) Others, Who _____

2 – Am I impressed by this person's life or ways?

( ) Yes   ( ) No

3 – Do I want to be like him/her?

( ) Yes   ( ) No

4 – Do I love or like this person?

( ) Yes   ( ) No

5 – Does this person love or like me?

( ) Yes   ( ) No   ( ) I don't know

6 – Do I admire or respect this person?

( ) Yes   ( ) No

7 – Does this person add value to my life?

( ) Yes   ( ) No

8 – Does this person appreciate me?

( ) Yes   ( ) No   ( ) I don't know

9 – What type of energy do I feel around this person?

( ) Positive   ( ) Neutral   ( ) Negative

10 – Does this person feel happy when I achieve something good?

( ) Yes   ( ) No

* If you would like to answer, "I don't know" to this question, the answer is "No", you would know if they were happy for you.

11 – Does this person often put me

( ) Up   ( ) Down

12 – When I do something, do I consider what this person will think?

( ) Yes   ( ) No   ( )Sometimes

13 – How much power does this person's opinion and judgment have in my decisions?

( ) None   ( ) Low   ( ) Medium   ( ) High

Now take a look at your answers, and you will have a better understanding of the weight of these people's opinions and judgments on your decisions.
The good news is that we can't please everyone, so you can already save your time and shake that responsibility off your shoulders.

Only listen to the ones who really matter, but even then, if the ones who matter are limiting you from being your best self, they will have to be ignored too.

We need to learn to separate things, your life belongs to you; other people can have an impact on your decisions, but they can't decide for you. At the end of the day, it is your life, and they can do whatever they like with theirs.

Give the right amount of attention to the people who you can learn from, the ones who have something interesting to offer, the ones who can help to bring out the best in you, and the ones who will still respect you even if you decide not to follow their advice.

Some people really care and try to protect you because they think they know best or they have failed in what you are trying to do, so they will try their best to prevent you from following in their footsteps.

They have good intentions and may have a hard time understanding why you want to go against their opinion, but they need to respect that, in the end, the decision comes from you as they can't live your life for you.

If they can't understand or don't respect your views, you will need to draw a line and make it clear that they can still support you without interfering, as you are not going to abandon your dreams to live theirs.

They may resist it for a while but, they will soon enough accept your position and respect you more for standing up for yourself and fighting for your goals.

Then there are other people who just don't want you to succeed because they aren't brave enough to do it themselves and will do everything they can to make sure you don't do it either.

They may come up with negative comments disguised as good advice on how and why you shouldn't go for it. They don't think you are capable, or if they do, they won't tell you because it pains them to imagine your success.

We need to keep in mind that what people think of us is their own business, it is the way they perceive the world. Our view of others is shaped by our own experiences and preconceptions.

Kind people see kindness in others; interesting people see interesting things in others; and the argumentative and negative person sees the same in others.

Sometimes it is hard to go against their opinion, especially if they are close and dear to us, but people treat us the way we allow them to, so if you feel that their judgment is prejudicial, you will need to stop accepting their negativity and then make it clear that their judgment won't change your decision.

At first, they may resist it because they are used to influencing your decisions, but you only need to put them in their place a couple of times for them to take a step back and start respecting you more.

We can still be friends and maintain a good relationship with people who aren't compatible with our ideas and plans, as long as we can ensure that they don't cross the line.

We need to protect our dream and keep on fighting for it until we get where we want. It isn't easy, and that's why so many people never do it.

Now let's talk about self-confidence which is the skill that lets you believe in yourself. You know you won't let yourself down, and you are secure in the knowledge that you will do your utmost to accomplish what you are working for.

> *Henry Ford once said: "Whether you think you can, or you think you can't, you're right."*

> *Steve Jobs once said: "The people who are crazy enough to think they can change the world are the ones who do."*

These quotes emphasize the power of self-confidence in achieving goals. Only the ones who have it will be brave enough to take action, while the others won't even try as they don't believe they can do it.

For some people, self-confidence doesn't come naturally ,but that isn't a problem because, with a decision and some work, it can be acquired.

I intentionally used the word "decision" because that is the essential element for all choices.

Decision comes in front of everything we do after consideration and gives us the basis for a choice of taking action or not.

In other words, we think, and then we select between alternatives.

When we choose something, we consider all alternatives and pick the ones we consider to be the best for what we have in mind.

How does that apply to self-confidence?

It applies to self-confidence and everything we do; we make so many choices every day, simple and complex, from what to wear to important steps towards achieving goals.

In the simple task of deliberately choosing to increase your self-confidence, you will notice various important decisions and choices.

Decision: Address the issue of low self-confidence.
Choice: Be open minded to learn what can be done.

Decision: Put in the effort towards the necessary steps and follow through.
Choice: What steps to take.

Decision: Recognize weak points.
Choice: What characteristics to obtain.

As you can see, decisions and choices are interconnected, and being aware of both is very helpful when you are on a mission for self-improvement.

"One day or day one, you decide" Unknown Author

Here comes another task for you:

TASK 6:

Use the space provided to write about your best qualities and character traits; they can be anything that pops into your mind; they don't need to be related to your goal.

Example: I am: funny, a good friend, reliable, honest, hardworking, have beautiful eyes, easy going, chilled, can keep secrets, kind, loyal, etc.

Now use this space to list your worst qualities and character traits.

Again, it can be anything that pops into your mind, it doesn't need to be related to your goal.

Example: I am: judgmental, insecure, pessimistic, lazy, ugly, annoying, shy, impatient, rude, negative, indecisive, etc.

And finally, use this space to write the character traits that you would like to have:

Example: resilience, perseverance, leadership skills, self-confidence, energetic personality, charisma, positive attitude, intelligence, self-control, etc.

It is possible to pick and choose the character traits that we wish to have.

TASK 7:

1 – Go back to task 6 and read out loud the list of character traits that you want to acquire.

( ) - Done

2 – You probably know people who have these characteristics, so make a list with as many names as possible. It could be someone that you know, a public figure or just anybody from the present or the past.

3 – Learn from these people's journeys, their stories and achievements, find out what they read, who inspired them and what they do, make them your role models; and take what you can from their experiences.

Use the space below for your notes:

4 - Use this space to write down a definition for what each one of these characteristics means to you, literally first and then personally.

For illustration, here is an example: Resilience

Literally: Ability to recover from difficulties.

Personally: I'll be strong enough to bounce back when things go wrong, and use the experience as a lesson. I won't give up.

"The most difficult thing is the decision to act, the rest is merely tenacity." Amelia Earhart

10. CHARACTER BUILDING

Allsuccessful people have something in common, and one of them is self-discipline.

There will be plenty of people who already have the dream that you are working towards.

When you look at these people, what do you see?

What personal characteristics can you spot on them?

Were they lucky?

In a sense, yes, but not for the obvious reasons, as nobody can achieve and maintain success purely based on luck.

The secret to maintaining your achievements and keeping on growing takes a lot more than just luck; it requires commitment, motivation, resilience, discipline and a lot of hard work.

If you decide to give it a go, while you ponder the habits that you want to acquire, let's talk about self-discipline.

What is self-discipline?

It is the ability to control your actions through conscious and consistent effort regardless of your emotional state, or, in other words, to make yourself do what you have decided to do deliberately and persistently even if you don't feel like it.

If you combine self-discipline with your plan of action you will be on the right path to achieving any goal that you want.

What if I still can't do it?

Then you will need to practice achieving smaller goals until you have more confidence to apply the process for bigger plans and progress to the next level.

Try creating a new habit and putting it to the test for 66 days. It can be something unrelated to your main goal, so try something not too difficult and see how it goes.

For example, in case you don't already do it, you could try drinking eight glasses of water a day. Put some alarms or apps on your phone to help remind you and do it every day, no matter what. Be committed to it; bring water with you when you go somewhere where it could be hard to find; make it a priority, and do not skip a day. If you do, then start again from the beginning. The secret is doing it repeatedly for 66 days consecutively, and by the end of it, you will have the habit of drinking eight glasses of water a day.

Removing distractions is an important factor when you are working on improving self-discipline, so get rid of anything that may divert your attention from your goal.

In our example of acquiring the habit of drinking eight glasses of water a day, it would be advisable to only have water available to drink; remove fizzy drinks, coffee, tea and any other temptations from your convenient reach until your old habits are broken and a new one takes place.

Nobody requires any of these drinks for survival; even the coffee drinkers who swear by only functioning after sipping their awakening elixir don't rely on coffee as much as they have made themselves believe.

Once the new habit is established, your water will be there next to all other drinks and you will be effortlessly choosing the water over anything else that is available.

When you realize the power of this exercise, as long as you are committed to self-discipline, you will feel more confident in applying it to any other habits that you wish to acquire.

Soon enough, you will have all those great habits on your list and more, because by thinking differently, you will act differently and consequently achieve differently. You will become more assertive and aware of your self-worth and power, and when you reach your goal you will wish you had done this sooner.

But hey, don't beat yourself up, it is better late than never.

What is a habit?

It is a behaviour pattern related to the way we act, think ,and react to things, events, and circumstances, often and repeatedly without thinking due to conditioning. It is like being on autopilot, acting unconsciously, and it feels like second nature.

If you want to find techniques to consciously develop new habits, you will have a lot to choose from. This kind of information is widely available to whoever is searching for it; you can buy books, listen to podcasts, watch YouTube videos, search the internet, and so on.

Having a variety of techniques is a great thing; however, I can only endorse the ones that I have tried and approved from experience.

What is self-esteem?

Contrary to self-confidence which means that you are secure about yourself and believe in your abilities, self-esteem is related to your acceptance of yourself. How much do you like yourself?

People with low self-esteem tend to be very cruel to themselves;

they don't like what they see in the mirror, and they don't like the way they are on the inside either.

If you read your three lists from this last task, you will have a better understanding of your level of self-esteem.

It isn't uncommon for people to be unhappy about certain traits that they have, and that's fine; it happens to most of us.

The reason why I brought up the self-esteem card is because, although totally different, it is very related to self-confidence which is our topic of interest at the moment.

People with low self-esteem can have low self-confidence because they don't believe in their abilities and are not happy about themselves, but you can be confident and still have low self-esteem.

For you to be able to work on the character traits that you want to acquire or improve, you will need to ask yourself if this judgment comes from yourself or from others.

It is important to learn from other people's feedback. You can observe if their perception of you is fair, and if you think it is, you can always improve.

If the judgment comes from others but is unfair, then it is their business and you don't have anything to do with it; problem solved.

People can think whatever they want about you, but you know your conscience and your values, and if they are honourable, stick to them, and you will never have to justify anything.

However, if the judgment comes from yourself, then you have something to work with.

For this purpose, let's focus on the list of characteristics that you would like to acquire. (Task 6)

The reason why I start with this list is because, when you learn new things, you become a different person, your mind and whole-body chemistry change. Later you will notice that your list of unwanted traits may become obsolete.

Another reason is based on the belief that it is more efficient to focus on what you want to achieve rather than spend valuable energy on what you want to eliminate.

To work on self-esteem, first it is necessary to change your mindset.

Mindset is your mental attitude, which determines your outlook on circumstances and situations; your perception is your reality.

You probably heard about the example of a glass being described as half full or half empty by different people, and that is a typical example of how one's mindset affects one's perception.

When you encounter difficulties, do you see it as a challenge or a curse?

While some people would agree that life has its ups and downs and start analysing the problem in search of solutions, others would feel defeated, thinking that only bad things happened to them because they were unlucky, and the world is unfair.

Both interpretations of the exact same problem are a reflection of a mindset.

Your mindset is a result of a habit, the habit of thinking in a certain way. You can train yourself to have a more positive mindset, if you make a conscious decision to change.

You will need to make an effort to think in a different way. Do it through being analytical, using positive visualization and affirmations, confronting your thoughts, practising gratitude, and being open and aware of possibilities and opportunities.

When a new obstacle appears in your way, instead of turning your back on it, you will look it in the eyes and take the challenge with an open mind, remembering that you will be enriched despite the outcome. Aim to win by doing your very best.

There is an inspiring old story by an unknown author that illustrates the perception of adversity:

A young lady went to her grandmother and told her how much she was struggling with her life problems. She was discouraged and very close to giving up.

Her grandmother invited her to the kitchen where she put on three pots of water to boil.

In the first pot, the old lady put in some carrots; in the second some eggs; and in the third, some coffee beans.

After boiling for about 20 minutes, she took everything out and asked the girl to tell her what she could see.

The girl replied, "Carrots, eggs and coffee, what does it mean?"

The old lady asked her to feel the three items.

The girl then noticed that the carrots went from hard to soft, the egg from soft and fragile to hard, and finally she tasted the coffee with its rich aroma and smiled.

Her grandmother explained that all three items faced the same challenge, which was the boiling water, but each reacted differently.

The carrot went in strong and rigid but came out soft and weak.

The egg was very fragile when t was placed in the boiling water, but its inside became hard.

However, the coffee beans were unique as they changed the water.

"Which one are you?" asked the grandmother, encouraging the girl to think about turning difficulties to her advantage.

Be grateful for difficult times as they are important for making you grow. Think of the possibilities involved in the process of solving a problem; perhaps you will need to learn a new skill, find new resources, or contact different people who can help. In doing so, you will be taking important decisions, and at the end of the task, you will be proud of your efforts. If the outcome was unexpected, you can still be proud of having learned another way that didn't work and keep on trying until you find a successful way.

> *"Never let a stumble be the end of your journey." Unknown author*

> *"I have not failed; I've just found 10,000 ways that won't work." Thomas A. Edison*

> *"Our greatest weakness lies in giving-up. The most certain way to succeed is always to try just one more time." Thomas A. Edison*

Keep on practising these techniques, and if you do it enough times, the new approach to problems will become a new habit for solving them. The more you practice, the easier it gets, so when you least expect it, you will have developed a habit of thinking differently.

If you carry out some research, you will see that many studies have been undertaken in this field. I noticed that a common observation is that you need at least 66 days to develop a new habit.

Neuroplasticity explains that the brain changes its neural pathways with new behaviour, which is why things get easier the more we practice.

With science backing us, we can trust, that just as in a computer, we can programme our brain to introduce and install new habits and behaviours into our lives. The more we use that process, the more conditioned we will be until it becomes second nature.

Think of all the things that you do on "autopilot", without effort, you always do it in the same way.

Here is an example that happened in my own house recently:

We bought a bigger fridge, so we had to rearrange the kitchen cupboards to make it fit. I can't tell you how many times all of us went to the washing machine when we wanted to get to the fridge only to realize that it wasn't there.

It wasn't a surprise to anyone that our kitchen looked different, as the change was obvious and we knew where everything was. However, we kept on repeating our old habit for quite some time until our brains created a new pathway and we finally stopped looking for milk in the washing machine.

Have you had a similar experience?

The same can happen to our way of thinking as we get used to thinking in a certain way and keep on repeating it until we decide to change.

If you decide that you want to improve your self-esteem and acquire new habits, you will need to put in the work.

Check your "to do" list from task 6 and 7 and dedicate your energy and full attention to act upon it.

With commitment to follow it through, you will automatically improve your self-confidence as a consequence of this process.

Don't forget to celebrate when you accomplish something; offer yourself some type of reward for every time you tick something off your list, as you will deserve it.

Self-rewards are more powerful than they get credit for, as they keep motivation at a high level due to the release of dopamine, a brain chemical associated with many roles, including pleasure and excitement.

Celebrating your own achievements is a recognition of your efforts, it reinforces positive behaviour and attitude and makes you feel proud and inspired to carry on aiming high towards goal achievement.

Rewards are symbolic tokens; they don't need to be great expensive gifts, but a little something that represents recognition and appreciation.

To illustrate the power of symbolic tokens as rewards, let's talk about smartwatches and fitness trackers that are so popular nowadays.

Their features allow you to set daily goals for how many steps you take, how much water you drink, exercise times, calorie intake, heart rate and so on.

From my own experience, I'd like to mention that I am often chasing my tail to complete the 10,000 step target so I can get a green star on my dashboard. It also encourages me to go the extra mile because I am an overachiever and hate to see my picture at a lower rank than my friends on our fitness group, and I know that my competitive friends do the same.

Healthy competition is fun; it encourages us to do more, but keep in mind that your biggest competitor in whatever you do is yourself, as you can always improve.

You can use others for reference, but do not compare yourself to them, as everyone has their own journey, and it is not fair to compare someone's end result to yours without knowing the trajectory that took them to where they are now.

Don't envy or despise people; everyone's position in life is a result of their choices and efforts.

Success or failure is more than a fair result; it is a consequence ruled by the law of action and reaction, which works equally for all.

"Diligence is the mother of good luck" Benjamin Franklin

11. GRATITUDE

The final chapter is purposefully titled "Gratitude."

I have many reasons for being grateful. One in particular is for you who read my first book to the end and found its contents valuable for your life. This will automatically do the same to mine, as the main purpose was to shed light on things that made a positive difference for me.

This book is a result of a dream, both literally and figuratively.

One day I woke up with a whisper; it was my kind inner voice loudly saying that I should write about my experiences with the techniques described here as they could be helpful to someone who might be looking for such words.

Then I had a figurative dream about already having the book ready and reading reviews of happy readers who had shared their insights with me on how it had helped or encouraged them to take action towards their goals.

For this book to become a reality, I went through every step mentioned. At the beginning, I only had an idea of the subjects that I wanted to write about. Since I had never written a book before, I wasn't sure if I would have enough inspiration to fill up a whole book that would captivate the reader's attention till the end.

Many times, in the process, I doubted myself, and with the help of my nasty inner voice, sometimes I thought I was going to be a laughing stock and I would never finish it or, if I did it, it would receive bad reviews and become a joke.

I confronted the negative thoughts and decided to go ahead and listen to the good ones. I had the support of my husband, who put up with my talking about it all the time and disappearing whenever I could to write some more.

His support and trust in me strengthened my confidence to keep on writing despite the fact that I can barely read what I write. I found a website that converts text into speech, and that was worth gold throughout the whole process as I could hear what I was writing as many times as I wanted.

The internet is so resourceful, and for that I am very grateful too.

Nowadays everything is so much easier; if you look for opportunities you will find them.

I'm sure this book won't be to everyone's taste; it would be pretentious of me to expect such a result but, in all honesty, I truly hope it will benefit some people.

There is an interesting thought about inspiration that I read somewhere. According to the Persian poet Rumi, whatever you seek is seeking you, and my understanding of this is that everything that is created came from inspiration.

Ok, that is easy to understand, but the wow factor of this theory is that all these creations wanted to be created and were whispered to the right person in search of revelation.

So, what you are looking for already exists somewhere and is also looking for you. As a matter of fact, I have an outstanding example of this theory, but for it to make sense, I need to give you another background story.

Back in 1999, I was still happy living with my grandmother, but I was going through some heavy disappointments in various areas of my life.

With six months until university graduation, I realised that I had chosen the wrong course for the second time, and although professionally I had a great job that I worked hard to achieve, I wasn't happy anymore. The worst part was that I was suffering from the end of another failed relationship.

Suddenly everything was going wrong all at the same time, and I just couldn't put my finger on what I was doing wrong.

At the time, most of my friends were starting families or were happy in relationships and although I was never alone for too long, I always felt lonely and disconnected.

In my mind, I thought that there was something wrong with me; my expectations for a relationship were so high that by the time I found my utopian love, if that ever happened, I would be too old to realise my dream of having a family.

Many times in life, I came to a crossroad where I had to decide whether to stay on the same path, conform, and stop complaining, or to take a chance on a new path to see where it would lead me.

At 26, there I was at another one of these crossroads, pondering whether to make a radical turn in my life or to continue in my comfortable position and accept the emptiness that I was feeling.

It took some time for me to balance my options; on one side I had a safe port, which was my good job and my grandmother with her endless source of love and support, and on the other side I had the desire for unknown things. At that point, I didn't know what it was, but I just felt as if I had to go away on my own somewhere as far away as possible.

I didn't know then, but later I came to understand that I wanted to escape from the pain of feeling personal inadequacy and loneliness.

I decided to radically change everything, starting with my appearance. I got a short haircut and became blond, a shocking change that made me cry for a while, but I enjoyed it later, even if just for a while, because blond hair really doesn't suit me.

I couldn't recognise myself in the mirror, and I was happy about that.

A few days later, I decided that I wanted to go far away with no rush to come back, and then, after some research, I got interested in becoming an air stewardess with the goal of travelling long and far.

Again, I went through the steps in this book. I found a company that I wanted to work for, discovered what their requirements were, and went to get the qualifications one after another.

After completing a five month course, I went through the practical part, which included a few days of jungle and sea survival as well as firefighting training, and then I passed the tough exam that gave me the legal document of a fully qualified professional.

With everything in hand, I passed the tests for the company that I wanted to work for, but they thought that my English had to improve, so they gave me the opportunity to retain my results, and if I came back with better English in three months, the job was mine.

Now what happens next is the inexplicable chain of events and "coincidences" that brought me to where I am today.

The story is a bit long, but I'll try to make it brief without losing the point, which is, **"what you look for is also looking for you."**

I was excited to have this job opportunity and took on the challenge to improve my English in three months. In my mind, the only way for such fast learning would be an intensive course in a country with English as its native tongue.

So, I balanced my options and chose the furthest possibility; I bought a ticket to Melbourne, Australia, with three months return to Brazil.

The plan was clear, and once again I had a vision of every step that I wanted to take in order to come back with better English and fulfil that job offer.

It took a while to organise my visa, the school and where to stay in Australia, and since I didn't want to come back to the same life, I sold my car, computer, telephone, clothes, bike and also donated a lot of things.

I could literally say that everything I owned was with me and in me.

It felt a bit scary at the beginning, but then it became liberating, and the more I got rid of things the lighter I felt.

I remember my grandmother standing at my bedroom door with a sad look on her face saying that I was leaving, never to come back.

At the time, I said that I was going to come back and rebuild my life from scratch, but I never stopped thinking about her words and how right she was.

When everything was ready and organised, the only thing missing was a certificate of vaccination requested by the Australian authorities for all Brazilians entering their country.

I was so excited for the big day to arrive, and with only four days until my long-awaited departure, I went to a hospital for the vaccine, but at the hospital's door I was hit by a speeding and uncontrollable car.

I have no memory of this event. I was told by my friend and some other witnesses that a speeding car lost control when the driver went over the speed bump while trying to avoid hitting an old lady crossing the road. He hit me instead, as I had just stepped out of the car and had my back to the road while closing the door.

The car hit me on the side and made me fly quite a distance until I fell onto another parked car and then landed motionless and unconscious on the road.

My friend who saw everything, was sure that I was dead.

The car tried to escape but was blocked by an oncoming truck; what type of person would do that?!

Luckily, I was at the right place and people from the hospital were quick to take me in.

I woke up six hours later very surprised to see so many people from my family around me. I didn't know where I was, and I didn't know what had happened.

Nothing was hurting until I tried to sit up on the bed, and I felt horrible pain all over my body. It was hard to breathe, and when I touched my hair, I noticed that my forehead was bleeding and that there was some glass stuck in my hair. I asked why everyone was there, and then, as if in a slow-motion scene of a movie, things started to make sense.

They told me what happened, and I was surprised to have any memory of any of it; I didn't feel any pain until I regained consciousness.

The accident was very costly for me as I had cancelled my health insurance a month prior to the trip. Consequently, I had to pay a lot of money for the hospital care, which included a few days stay and a surgery. It left me with a broken pelvis, a broken collar bone, an exposed finger fracture, some broken ribs, broken teeth and countless bruises all over.

As you can imagine, I was devastated that I had the annoying accident after having everything so meticulously planned for my trip. I felt literally broken.

While at the hospital, I decided that I wouldn't be stopped by the accident, and with the help of a friend, I managed to postpone my departure until four months later. I had to recover within that period, no matter what.

The driver who hit me and tried to run away was lucky that I decided not to prosecute him. It would have been too time-consuming as I was so immobile and would have had to spend time and energy with a lawyer, court, and so on.

Instead, I concentrated on my recovery. My grandmother was like an angel, looking after me with so much care. I was bedridden for a long time, then I went on to use a wheelchair and crutches, and then four months later, with some difficulties, I could finally walk again. Just as I had planned, there I was, boarding a plane to Australia.What an amazing feeling!

I landed in Melbourne with a 32 kg suitcase and 10 kg of hand luggage, which was all I had. It was so exciting that I felt like an explorer.

There in Australia, I learned a lot, but after nearly three months, I realised that my English wasn't good enough, so I contacted the company to say that I needed more time and, to my surprise, they told me that they were happy to wait another three months.

I couldn't believe my luck and went straight to the embassy to extend my visa for another three months.

In the six month period, I travelled, had various odd jobs, from waitressing to gardening, and had lots of fun. After six months, I wasn't sure if I still wanted to go back to the job anymore.

I wanted to stay longer and travel around as much as I could until my visa expired, and then I'd return to Brazil and start again. I was confident that it would be easier with good English, so I extended my visa for another three months, and just like that, I stayed for nine months.

It was worth every minute, I made great friends, learned a lot, and had lots of fun.

At home, I was forever preoccupied with fitting in and was always searching to feel complete in the company of others, but in Australia I had a different purpose. I was there to learn and have fun; for the first time my main focus was myself, and I discovered that I am good company for myself. I spent so much time on my own that I learned to enjoy my own company, and in doing so, I attracted more interesting people into my life.

Travelling alone is a great way to discover yourself. There were lonely times, but they were not sad.

There I needed so little. As long as I had a place to sleep and some food to eat, I was happy, and by expecting so little, everything that came my way was greatly appreciated.

When the nine months in Australia came to an end, my return ticket to Brazil had a stop in New Zealand.

While living in Australia, I had been to New Zealand once before for a very short trip just to extend my visa for the next three months. Although I had a good feeling for the place, at the time I didn't have any money to stay and enjoy the trip, so I had put it into my bucket list for when I found an opportunity, and now was the time.

I was a bit sad to go back home and wanted to extend my trip to its maximum because I knew that when I was back in Brazil, things would get a bit tough until I settled into a new life.

I could stay in New Zealand for three months, and I rationed how much money I could spend each day. My intention was to find a casual job and stretch my stay for as long as possible so that I could travel around that beautiful country.

I had booked myself to stay at Bamber House, a good budget hostel in Auckland where I had stayed once before.

The office was closed when I arrived late in the night, but a friendly guy came to let me in and showed me the room. I liked him so much that I couldn't quite concentrate on anything he was saying, but he never noticed that.

That night, I realised that I had left a bag in the shuttle bus. I was sad about that because all the letters that my grandmother had sent to me were in that bag, together with some books and pictures.

The next day, I went to the office and asked the handsome guy if he could try to locate the bag for me as I was traveling to the South Island the next day. I would return there if he found it, as my ticket to Brazil would depart from Auckland.

He promised to do his best to find it, and for this reason I gave him my e-mail, and I invited him for lunch as I had a frozen lasagne, which seemed to be enormous for one person.

He agreed to share my lasagne, and it was funny to realise that most of it was packaging and the actual lasagne was tiny.

Anyway, over lunch, we had a good time chatting. I felt sorry to leave the place, as I would've enjoyed spending more time with him.

He gave me lots of tips and advice on where to stay and what to see in the South Island. He understood that I was travelling on a budget and arranged for me to stay at the house of one of his friends in Christchurch for a fraction of the price that I would have paid at the hostel I had in mind.

There at Fiona's house, I had a good time. She was a fun lady, and we got along very well, so we even went travelling together.

For the whole period that I stayed with her, she was always telling me what a nice guy Marcus was and how he liked to fix and improve everything in the house.

She thought we would make a good couple because we were very alike as I was always cleaning the house, working in the garden and cooking nice Brazilian food for us. She kept on saying that we should get to know each other a bit more.

I explained to her that I really liked him but had only spoken to him briefly because we met one day, and I went away the next. Also, that I was about to return to Brazil, so I didn't think much of it at all.

There in Christchurch, I went out every day trying to find a job but couldn't find anything as it was low season and my rationed money was running out quite quickly.

I went to the library to check my email and had a message from Marcus saying, "Hey, I haven't found your bag yet, but how are you doing?"

We started exchanging messages, and I told him that I was enjoying it there but that I only had a few more days to find a job or I would have to go back to Brazil in six days' time.

He then told me that, I could work as a cleaner at Bamber House for two and a half hours a day in exchange for accommodation and have the rest of the day to find a job. He also said that because of his contacts, he could take me to swim with dolphins and go black water rafting for free.

I promise you that I didn't need all that to convince me, and I went to a travel agency the very next day and bought a ticket to Auckland.

Marcus came to pick me up at the airport. He was even more handsome than I could remember, and he took me to Mount Eden to see the amazing view of the night sky and city lights.

In the following days, we worked in the morning, and then I walked all day looking for a job, and in between things, we went out on our adventures as he had promised.

Everything was going well, but without a job, I only had three more days to stay. On the very last day, I found a job as a waitress and kitchen hand in a French restaurant.

There was a very slim chance that I could stay longer. The restaurant paid a fair wage, and I would complement my earnings with tips and by making a chocolate mousse pie to sell to the same restaurant. As the waitress, every time I was serving at the tables, I would suggest that dessert to anyone who would listen.

I considered it as a success; the owner of the restaurant was very happy with my service, and I started to work every day at lunch and then again at dinner. As I could eat at work, I even managed to save some money for more travels.

Meanwhile, things with Marcus were going well although, I had to ask for a kiss because he was too respectful, and after that we became inseparable.

After nearly four months in New Zealand, the time had finally come for me to leave because I couldn't extend my visa any further.

I told Marcus that I had a plan to return to Brazil, work for six months and then go to Switzerland for my cousin's birthday because I had promised it to her.

He then told me that he would follow me wherever I went.

I couldn't believe it but told him that he was welcome to come with me if he wanted to.

Then we decided to exchange my return ticket for an around-the-world ticket, and Marcus bought the same for himself. Our tickets included several stops in different countries of our choice.

We travelled for one whole year together and had many interesting experiences in various countries like Thailand, Greece, Germany, Sweden and Switzerland, where we got married one year later. We then went on to Argentina, Brazil and then back to New Zealand again.

Altogether, we travelled for about two years until we decided to settle down in England. The plan was to work there for two or three years and save enough money to start a hostel business in Brazil.

We found a live-in job as a couple and kept on extending the years while we managed to save enough money to buy a piece of land for our dream business in Brazil. After six years, we became parents to our first son, so we decided to stay longer in order to save money for a house for us to live in while building the hostel. We had to be a bit more cautious to make sure we could provide and fulfil the needs of our little family, so we decided to stay just a bit longer until we could save for a second house that we could rent and generate some income from.

We then had our second boy in 2008. We were delighted that we finally had everything we needed, but the recession that year caused our savings to lose so much of their value that we ended up with less money than we would have had if we had gone the previous year.

That was a big blow to our plans, and we were placed together as a family in another one of life's crossroads where we had to search for a plan B, which at the time we didn't have.

In moments like that, I always ask the universe for help. I prayed for clarity of thoughts, and then the answer came quickly and from an unexpected source.

In a conversation with our boss at the time, he suggested, "Why not buy a house here instead?"

We never imagined settling in the UK, let alone buying a house here, because we didn't think we could afford it.

Becoming a parent is something that changes you. While before we only thought about having a job that would allow us to live in a tropical country by the beach, we started thinking about the children's future, and after balancing the opportunities they would have in the UK compared to Brazil, staying was an easy decision.

As you can see, so much has happened since I decided to leave Brazil as the start of a new life.

So many times, things didn't go according to plan, and now, looking back, we can pinpoint all the lucky misfortunes that brought us together and helped us became the happy family I had always dreamed of since I was a little girl.

In conclusion, I'd like to go back to that interesting point in Rumi's philosophy that says, **"Whatever you seek is also seeking you."**

Back when I was at home, following my grandmother's advice, I used to go to an old lady called Dona Laura who prayed for people. Every time she prayed for me, she said that one day I was going to find a very good husband who would love me dearly, but he was very far away, and I remember being annoyed with her because I didn't ask for her predictions and I didn't believe that she was able to know that, but I kept going back there from time to time because my grandmother wanted me to.

So many times, when I had a boyfriend and thought it would be the one, she would tell me that my perfect husband would still be far away, and I remember swearing at her in my thoughts. Considering what I know now, I hope she didn't notice that.

The first time I went to Brazil with Marcus we were already married, and Dona Laura came by and prayed for me. We didn't mention anything to her, but as soon as she started, she looked at me with such a surprised reaction and told me, "You found him."

It was only then that I started having some respect for her predictions, and to this day I still don't understand how she could have known.

It makes me wonder if our lives are predestined when we have a clear picture of what we want while wishing for that something so deeply in our soul that the object of our dream, if matched with the frequency of wishing for it, finds its way to us.

My main goal in life has always been to be part of a happy family. This was my deepest desire, and although I wasn't aware of it, every step and every decision I took led me to it.

I used to write in early journals about the type of father I wished I had, and how I hoped my mother would protect me when I needed it.

Now I see that we became the family of my dreams, and I am so grateful to my parents for having helped me to build that dream in every little detail.

Every day I deliberately tell my children that they are important. Sometimes they even get annoyed, but I do it anyway because they really are.

I feel blessed beyond words to be able to enjoy family life at last and especially to make my children feel loved and appreciated.

Now looking back, it's ironic that I'm grateful for all the lucky misfortunes that shaped my life into what it is today.

The magical power of forgiveness is something that we don't want to miss out on.

There is nothing worse than feeling painful resentment towards somebody who did us wrong, especially if that somebody is unaware of what they did or is not sorry.

We don't need to forget to be able to forgive. In fact, it is good that we don't forget because of the valuable lessons that come from experiences.

Forgiveness is not something you do for others; you do it for yourself.

You've probably heard of Buddha's quote that says, "Holding onto anger is like drinking poison and expecting the other person to die."

It helps if we take a step back to analyse the situation while acknowledging that our frustration comes from our own unfulfilled expectations.

People live by their own values, and they act and interact accordingly. You can't expect them to give what they don't have.

For that reason, it is better if you focus on yourself and decide how you are affected by external interactions; if you take everything as a lesson, you will feel grateful even when it is painful.

Don't allow other people's "ugly" to spoil your essence; their problem is not with you, it is with themselves. They can only affect you negatively if you allow them to.

Thinking this way will help you to detach from the problem and make it easier for you to forgive the poor person who is missing out on living their best life.

I learned to love my parents for who they are. It is a bit sad that we have a gap between us, but I wouldn't change it for the world. They were my pillars in life, and even when it was painful or for the wrong reasons, they were my greatest source of inspiration for most of my achievements in life.

Another great misfortune was the car accident that delayed my trip to Australia. If I had left four months earlier, I would have missed meeting Marcus, as he wouldn't yet have been there. This is only my side of the story; on his side, there were loads of lucky misfortunes too.

The chances for us to meet were so slim, but somehow everything fell perfectly into place.

My understanding of this whole story is that there is a frequency that connects people with similar vibration. We were from opposite sides of the world, but we were looking for the same thing, and the universe conspired to bring us together.

Was it meant to be? We will never know, but I like to think it was.

Remember the bag with my grandmother's letters that I forgot on the shuttle bus?

It was the reason why I had to give my email address to Marcus, and later we came to find out that the bag had been left at his office. One day, he decided to look inside that bag and noticed that it was mine. It had been there all along, so we count that as another lucky misfortune.

I'd like to end this book with a piece of advice to whoever is looking for these words.

You can turn pain into power!

Never lose hope of achieving your deepest desire, when everything goes wrong. Always remember that you are worth it, and as long as you believe in the dream that already exists inside you, despite adversities, through action you will find a way to manifest that dream, even if it takes a long time. DO NOT GIVE UP!!

"Gratitude turns what we have into enough." Unknown author

"Know that one day your pain will become your . Rumi

12. BONUS CHAPTER: SYNERGY

It is interesting to learn from the birth of ideas that become massive corporations, fantastic constructions, amazing expeditions, and other grand achievements.

For reference, search for the story of Coca-Cola or the steel business of Andrew Carnegie.

As Earl Nightingale once said: "Everything starts with an idea."

Think big and beyond your field of sight, discuss your ideas with likeminded people, create a support group, and take advantage of synergistic alliances.

A support group is formed by people who believe in you but not necessarily in your ideas. They are a great source of encouragement and support and their belief in you will keep you motivated.

The transition from idea to achievement involves many things. As we've been studying in this book, it is our responsibility to recognise the potential of our dreams. You may have an idea that could benefit others and be an asset to the world.

If you are sure about your idea and are open to discuss it with others, you may like to invite collaborators to share your vision.

So much can be attributed to the synergy of alliances which, in simple words, means that one mind plus another mind creates a brand new third mind.

It refers to the new ideas that are generated by the combination of the two minds and if you add more minds into the equation, the principles of synergy are guaranteed to produce more ideas.

A synergistic alliance is formed by people who embrace the vision and share the same ideal, coming from different backgrounds and contributing with their ideas and talents; their input combined with the input of other members of the alliance will converge to form a common goal.

The results you can achieve on your own can be great, but they can't be compared to the magnitude of contribution and collaboration of others.

Join forces with people who share your vision and can complement the skills you lack; the collective power of a sound and determined alliance is practically unbeatable.

Here are some of Andrew Carnegie's quotes on collaboration and the synergy of alliances:

> *"The secret of success lies not in doing your own work but in recognizing the best person to do it."*

> *"No man will make a great leader who wants to do it all himself or get all the credit for doing it."*

> *"No man becomes rich unless he enriches others."*

These quotes highlight the phenomenal power of synergy and

collaboration in transforming dreams into reality for the greater good.

You can add many people to help you in pursuing your dream, either working for you or working with you, and all are equally important as long as you are clear when sharing your philosophy and plans.

A team where each individual plays on the same side for a common goal is worth its weight in gold.

If you have a "golden team", look after them well, as they deserve appreciation and recognition to keep motivated.

In a "golden team," everyone is strong, performing their best at any given task, and understanding the cycle of growth. If they grow, the company will grow and viceversa.

If your dream is to start a business, think of how much each member of your team can contribute and how valuable they are, and pay them accordingly.

Select them well, don't scrimp, and go for the best you can afford. You've probably already heard the expression "pay peanuts and get monkeys."

In the long run, hiring a non-professional individual can end up more expensive than paying an expert.

By "expert", I don't mean only academically prepared individuals; there are a lot of people out there with extraordinary talents and experiences. Don't judge a book by its cover; give people a chance; listen to whoever makes an effort to become noticeable to you; they may have all the potential of a rough diamond, so consider them too when you are searching for your golden team.

Strong leadership is indispensable, so make sure your whole team understand the vision, goals, and mission of your business. You need to have clear plans that make your targets achievable to keep your team inspired and motivated.

Invest in regular training, brainstorm meetings, and customers feedback reviews and act upon them to improve the quality of your products and services.

Your team members are assets, so at all times make them feel as important as they are, and they will perform beyond expectations.

Valuable individuals overperform because their main goal is not the money, although it may be important to them; but their goal is to contribute to a cause and grow with the company.

You may like to invest in expert advice for hiring valuable individuals, and you will get your money's worth every time.

The hierarchy of a business should keep their customers at the very top, they are the main reason businesses exist, therefore they come first.

Customers are the holy grail of any business and should be treated accordingly.

The next level of the hierarchy, which is equally important, is the group of people who deal directly with the customers. They are your sales front and customer service advisers, who will provide vital feedback about your customers' needs and preferences.

This valuable information can be worked upon to improve and adapt your products and services to better serve your customers.

Think of the low paid personnel who treat customers as an inconvenience and can't wait for the end of the day so they can go home.

This kind of employee can ruin a business in no time, so invest and choose carefully when you are employing someone.

Next on the hierarchy are your managers and supervisors, whose training should be focused more on the customers and employees than anything else.

Lastly come the executive management.

This type of structure is simply based on putting the needs of the customers first and then adapting the management to follow.

Most businesses are created to fill a gap in the market and provide products or services that are missing or that can be done differently or better.

At the beginning, the dream of good companies is to provide a great product or service to fully satisfy their customers.

Then some businesses grow so much that they lose touch with their customers. Things start to go wrong when their customers feel unappreciated and start fleeing to a competitor.

Treating customers with care and respect is crucial at all times, no matter how big your business grow, so if you want to keep and increase your position in the market, never forget the main reasons why you started your business, and maintain the focus on customers' satisfaction.

I've worked in sales for over 30 years, and from what I've experienced, I can tell you that a happy customer is an asset.

They will always come back to you, and they won't think twice about recommending you to anyone they think could benefit from your services or products.

Customer loyalty is valuable; don't break their trust, and they will happily pay even more just for the peace of mind of being able to count on you.

Focus on solving a problem or satisfying a necessity, combined with excellence in customer service, and your product or service will sell itself.

Apple is a good example of a great company that never fails to exceed its customers' expectations. For that reason, it is so successful that its loyal customers won't even look elsewhere for similar products and will pay handsomely for Apple's products based on the trust that they won't be disappointed with the product or service.

Even if you start a small business, learn from the world leaders as their hits and errors make great lessons, and if your goal is to get big, it is better to implement these lessons from the start.

Never get too comfortable in your position; the competition out there is fierce and will capitalise on your flaws.

Remember, none of these giant businesses were born that big, they were once inside someone's head, just like your idea is inside yours now.

They went through the process to stand strong where they are, and if you follow the steps, you can do it too.

"Earn your success based on service to others, not at the expense of others." H. Jackson Brown Jr.

" A business that makes nothing but money is a poor business." Henry Ford

ACKNOWLEDGEMENT

I would like to thank my lovely husband and best friend for his continued support and encouragement. He never complains when I wake him up in the middle of the night or the early hours to ask for his opinion about my crazy ideas.

Another big thank you to modern life and technology for providing limitless opportunities to people who are thirsty for knowledge and prefer to learn in their own way and at their own pace.

A massive thank you to Napoleon Hill and Jim Rohn, whose philosophies have greatly enriched my life. In my opinion, their work is one of the most precious gifts left to humanity. They are still inspiring millions of people all around the world long after their passing. May Mr. Hill and Mr. Rohn rest in peace.

ABOUT THE AUTHOR

Alice Miller

Alice was born and raised in Brazil, and as a result of her turbulent upbringing in a dysfunctional family, she acquired the habit of always having an escape plan.

She overcame heart attacks, accidents, bullying and so many other misfortunes which she has learned to be grateful for.

One day, at another one of life's crossroads, she bravely decided to leave her comfort zone, quit her job, sell everything that wouldn't fit in her suitcase, and move to Australia on her own. Carrying big dreams and a few belongings, she believed that she had everything she needed within herself.

She decided to write this book because turning pain into power is one of her talents. By outlining strategies for achieving goals and coping mechanisms that she has personally tested, she hopes to inspire others who may be feeling trapped by their circumstances to take action towards a happier and more fulfilling life.

"Every time I survive, only the weak part of me dies." Alice Miller

DISCLAIMER

The content provided in this book is intended to share helpful information, processes and techniques on the discussed subjects; they are endorsed by the author based on her own experience with all that is mentioned. All recommendations are made without guarantee on the part of the author; therefore, any liability in connection with the use of this information is disclaimed. If you need specific advice from a medical, legal or financial professional, please seek someone who is licensed and knowledgeable in that area.

Printed in Great Britain
by Amazon

13890324R00061